Hermit Season

Poems & Visions

by

Alix Klingenberg

This book is dedicated to my family, friends,
guides, and community.

And most especially to John, David, and Quillen,
who support me in so many ways and put up with
me disappearing for days to write.

And for my readers, of course; I couldn't do any
of this without you.

Initiate yourself into the world of magical things

Do not wait to be invited
into the center, be among
the circle and feel the power
of witness and participation
without needing to be the lead.

Let the sparrow have her say,
the elephant and the otter,
the blue whale will take its time,
be patient while the aspens
get their thoughts together.

Be present as the scribe,
the pattern-maker, the poet,
the artist, the seer,
and the song.

Poet Seer

She holds a small box in her hands at night, and inside are the stories only the moonlight can tell. She can't control the volume, and all the slides are out of order. Many of them belong to other people: ancestors, passers-by, alternate versions of herself. And the seer cannot parse or rewind, only receive, with half-hewn tools, and try to remember the tales in the morning.

House Cat Days

The cat is always crying,
and nothing seems to satisfy her.
I know how she feels,
a woman trapped in a house of comforts.

A wild huntress staring out the window,
waiting for her plate to be filled,
waiting for the kind of love
that makes it worth it,

that justifies her own captivity.

Jaguar Nights

I am a hunter
but I've lost my way again,
so I wait in the meadow
(where the tree is).

The black jaguar, (who is my guide),
sleeps silently at my side
and the fox walks the perimeter
so I can rest.

They remind me
that disorientation is part of the process,
but I am sleepless and resistant.

I can feel the new worlds
shifting beneath the surface and
I need to be alert,
not bracing for what's next,
but held and wise and ready.

The jaguar yawns and offers his back.
The fox returns from the edge
and nods to the cat.

A door opens with a crack
and a voice inside says,
it's time.

What is magic?

It is breath and silence.
Words with powerful intent.
The crackling energy between us.
The pull of the moon.
It is the call of the blackbirds
and the wind in the tall trees.
It is the whispering of first lines
and the quickening of the pen.
It is salt water and fresh sage.
It is secrets uttered into darkness.
It is the unexpected synthesis,
the alchemy of connections.
It is you, it is me, it is us.

Taurus Sun

Give me a cave,
a hole in the ground,
a stand of trees.

Become a stream running through me,
I will be the bedrocks
and the branches.

I Tried

I don't know how to explain
why I left the world behind,
why I disappeared

into the page, my bed, the inside
of my own skull, the woods.

Only that the world felt
like walking out of a movie
theater in summer, too bright.
an unwelcome, hostile landscape
of parking lots and Applebees.

Only that my own company
became a refuge,
a safe place after decades
of avoiding its quiet landscapes.

And some people will feel abandoned,
and some will wonder where I've gone
with a momentary brow raised.
Most won't notice - and that's ok.
That's how it ought to be, really.

Because we can't be everything
to everybody.
Believe me,
I tried.

What do you want?

I want to sit in the shade,
drink cold lemonade,
and snack on carrots from the garden.

I want to read a book
and tell someone how I like it.

I want a new secret or two,
nothing nefarious, just something
for me alone,
to remind myself
I exist
outside
of those I love.

Just a small space of
absolute privacy.

Cave of Arrows

It's not a definable fatigue,
it's so many things at once.

I forage for a thought
that moves in a straight line,
one that contains a beginning,
middle, and end,

but my mind is a cave of arrows,
an ever-expanding mass of particles,
bending around the black hole
that is my sense of self.

I try to tell you the truth,
but the same words are also a lie.

I draw you a map in three dimensions,
but you only see two,
and I turn to paper and ash,

just remnants of the whole
pinned to your chest,
edges raising with the breeze.

I take selfies when I'm depressed

Some days
I just need someone
to remind me
I exist.
That I am knowable
seeable
lovable.

The Midsummer Fairy

The Midsummer Fairy wakes after dark,
on the longest day of the year,
to share her wisdom and mischief with me.

She places plums in my pockets
and teaches me new ways
of playing human for another year.

We share our truths
and call them fiction,
we sing the same song
in our heads.

We dance wildly together,
under the strawberry moon,
while the trees pretend to sleep.

Litha

I am most myself when the sun sets at 9pm
and the crickets play their symphonies
deep within the purple clover.

I become the butter
slowly melting on the counter,
the freshly picked basil
sprinkled onto everything,
the cutting board full of ripe tomatoes
and goat cheese.

Dream Lemons

I dreamt of a cobalt bowl
overflowing with lemons,
but I didn't mean to buy two five-pound bags
in my online grocery order -
thought I was buying just two lemons.

This is how my dreams come true:
On accident. The multitudes of lemons
pooling in a yellow ball pit of joy on the
dining room table. An exact snapshot
stolen from my subconscious mind.

The next day, I got déjà vu in the car,
your arm hair touching my arm hair,
and suddenly we were children,
whispering secrets under a cobalt sky,
and I was pulled through a portal
of remembering.

Cowboys

You remind me of the best parts of my father
or perhaps you are a handheld mirror
to my own rugged, gambler heart.

I dream of horses lately, gray with mournful eyes
and soft hair. I am so often men in my dreams.

My hands so large and capable,
I am my grandfathers,
the rancher, the fiddler,
the minister, the horse-whisperer.

Never the women
with their tight lips
and lace collars. Only the men,
with their leather saddles
and tobacco pouches.

I live out this life with cowboys in my veins,
cowboys in my dreams.

My Roman Empire

They say men
think about the Roman Empire
more than you'd imagine,
but I wonder how often men think
of starting over
in a foreign town, alone.

New name. Fresh haircut.
A white button-down shirt
and straight-leg jeans.

Perhaps the orange lights
across the water beckon
them to a less disciplined
kind of territory,

a cherished softness,
a crisp, sun-bleached
future, billowing gently
in the afternoon breeze.

A New Archetype

Become the eccentric older woman
you've always been on the inside.

Wear outrageous clothes and live in a house
with jewel-toned rooms and magazines piled high,
art hung on the walls made by painters you knew
in your Parisian phase.

Show the world your collection of animal bones
and tarot cards, get a couple more cats,
a wolf pup you raise from birth,
swim naked in the dark and glistening waters.

Turn the page and leave everything known behind,

create a new archetype - one they'll tell their
children about, the one who didn't have to compromise,
the one who lived free
and stayed alive
and loved.

Why Poetry?

The purpose of poetry is to leave
something of this specific time.

To say, "Hey, I was here,
and my mind was afire
with love and peaches
and daisy chains.

My body was ripe with hiphop
and chocolate cake
and dogs barking.

This place was beautiful
and cruel and boring and long,
but here is a poem,
and something in it
is the truest thing
I can say right now.

Something in it means this life is real,
and now, and mine."

A song plays unexpectedly on Spotify

Sometimes despair
finds us, in the middle

of summer. The sprinkler
stills, the basil left
half-chopped on the cutting

board.

Buck Moon

The dog hasn't been out of the house
or yard for a couple of days
and I am aware that time is passing again.

The Earth is tilting quickly toward and away
from the Sun. The Moon is waxing
and waning, never standing quite
as still as the poets will have you believe.

I am a shade, a ghost again,
living twice on paper
but never really in the world.

I sit sweating on a chair,
propped up with pillows,
and my notebooks fill with ink
I'll never share.

It is that kind of summer,
empty and warm,
glowing with a soft crescent light
as I wait for something to shift
beneath me,

a fault line to open perhaps,
a bush to burn spontaneously -
a voice from above to task me
with some great purpose.

But the earth remains solid
beneath my bare feet and
the rain makes exploding foliage
unlikely.

For now, it's just me and this
July moon, sitting in near silence
together.

That kind of summer

I'm having a hard time.
It's all this beauty, you see,
it's breaking something inside me.
These summer days are
so brilliant they ache,

and my heart is too full,
far too full, for everyday things.

Brooding

I have tucked my grief
behind my ears,
I wear it on my wrists,
ask you to smell it.

Curl up with it like an egg
in fetal position,
the slight damp from the shower
creating a cold spot in the sheets.

I can't sleep.
I feel the pressure in the back
of my throat, and all I want
is to cry, and all I do is lie
prone and listen to the fake rain
coming from my phone.

I keep hoping someone will see
into this fog I'm in,
crawl in behind me
and this sad egg I'm guarding,
pry it free from me
or at least hold me
while I hold it.

Fallow

I turned to solitude,
to rest and recuperation,
not just from death
but also from life -
the friends I could no longer
meet with open hands,
the work that had served its purpose.

Everything fell away
until it was just me
and the hardwood floor,
just me and the cup of ginger tea,
just me and the old-growth forest,
just me and the inside of my memories.

Grief laid the field to rest,
the ground lay fallow and open,
ready for whatever might grow
in its wake.

Be here now

Make some art
move slowly
but move.
Follow through on obligations
but make fewer obligations.

The planets are scrambling my mind

Mars and Saturn square the sun,
or some such thing, and all I know

is my teeth have become a cage,
and my throat is sore
with the need to scream.

I cry instead.
I wail and moan

and finally the heat
inside me breaks
like a summer rain

and love floods my veins
like a newborn's smile,
reassuring me that the agony

of rebirth has given life
to something real.

Close

I want to write a story so close
that you know how it feels to hear my heart
pounding as I try to fall asleep at night,

the sound of the dog's crate closing,
the ticking of the chain on the ceiling fan.

I want you to feel my breath catch
when I remember how much I have,
how much I've lost,
and the grief of too much and too little

creeps in like the light from the neighbor porch,
spilling itself onto the unseasonable flannel sheets.

The Seeker

I keep thinking
I've come out of hiding
only to realize I'm still hiding.

Maybe I'm hiding more than ever.
I don't even know
what the opposite of hiding is.

Snow White

I write like a woman
who once got lost in the forest and found she was being hunted
by her stepmother for being too beautiful,
found solace in men who acted like children,
became a mother to anyone who could house her.

I write like a woman
who would poison an apple
and pretend to be ancient
to deceive a young woman to her ruin.

I often cannot tell if I am the heroine or the villain,
the ingénue or the axman staying his hand,
betraying his queen.

Perhaps I am the wolf, after all,
craving blood and meat and fullness,
needing the pack and also needing to roam
these mythic lands in utter solitude
until I can bury my teeth in your neck, shaking.

12 Dancing Princesses

To dance all night,
unwatched, unrestrained, unobserved.
To wear out our shoes and ask for more
without apology, without explanation.
This is the kind of freedom
every woman would lie for,
might let a man die for.
To simply exist in pleasure
without asking for permission.

Artifacts

I surround myself with beautiful things:
dried flowers and muted paint chips

vintage black-and-white film and used matches
photographs of myself in other places
smiling brightly with people I've loved

glass bottles and poetry books
tarot decks and textbooks about
why people are the way they are

earth-toned coffee mugs that fit in my palm
unframed works of art I have yet to hang

the remnants of joy
reminders of connection, creativity, peace
the artifacts of who I've been
and who I want to be.

Wiser

I don't usually want to drink,
but when I do, I want to drink
like I want to be 17 again,
wistful and impossibly aware
that it's not all it's cracked up to be.

I'm more unbridled now
than I was in my teen years,
more free and rebellious,
more artful, more defiant,

maybe even more beautiful
if you like your women wise
and strong and honest.

Matriarch

There's something about living
close to the sea
that makes you feel
like you might be able
to escape the patriarchy,

fall into the waves and disappear
into the mother
with her shark jaws
and endless fathoms,
free.

The Other World

It felt like folk music and candlelight,
like a circle of women drumming,
it felt like sage water and wisdom,
like clean sheets and the middle of a good book,

your mother doing dishes in the other room,
the cat washing her face in the morning light,
a fridge full of groceries and a quiet corner
just for you to write in.

The words fall out
like piano keys in a perfect new rhythm
only you can hear.

The trees are sentient and wise,
dressed in leaves and bark
showing you the way to an ancient set of secrets
they reserved just for you.

Hand-crafted, indigo-bound secrets
delivered in verse, in visions, in sleep.

The other world is there all the time,
knocking gently on the quiet places,
reminding you: You only need to close
your eyes or open the page.

River Song

She hums a tune
she's made up at the river,
holds my hand and pets my face;
our foreheads touch and I am
salt water and sunlight,
not a spot of humanity left,
just parts strung together
with minerals and memory.

Everything Good

Windows & Doors: an opening to breezes, cool and warm. I walk between worlds, the worlds change seasons, welcome me with lamp posts or walkways. Always a fire, always a tree.

Hands & Mouths: skin and skin and skin and tongue. Shark bodies, mountains and valleys, pulleys, magnets drawn close together. Sometimes teeth cut through softness, gasping red, the color of pleasure.

Stones & Rivers: the bedrock, foundations, the things that move and those that don't. The permeable moments and the hard dead ends. Always a decision to stand or to flow.

Keys & Flowers: the tangible, beautiful things. Ceramic bowls and orange slices, sourdough bread with butter. Your hair in my fingers, the grass under my toes, the sound of bees working, the high priestess card, a lioness.

Everything good that opens and closes, opens and closes.

Embodiment has its perks

Take the mountain pass
Roll the windows down
Tell the stories that make you speed up with joy
Run your fingers through their hair
and tell them you can't stop thinking of their smile
Be so honest people call it refreshing
Ease into the river until it carries your grief downstream
Be gentle with your energy
Take a bath and stand looking at the full
harvest moon before the heat wears off
Let yourself fall in love again
Let yourself be enough for that.

The Hum

My fingers have found the edges
of something so large
it's nearly impossible to fathom.

It has been sleeping for eons,
a rhythmic hum coming up
from deep within the earth,

so common to us all
we've tuned it out,
like the electric buzz of
fluorescent lights.

It rattles my teeth and
eats at my sanity, but I
seem to be the only one
who can feel it.

Can you feel it?

Chosen Family

We have built our family of honesty and sarcasm,
easy lounging, and snack dinners
of cheese and crackers, raspberries, and raw veggies.
We have built our family on music and board games,
on sleeping early and often, on saying "no"
to anything that hurts the soul.

In this family we tell the truth.
We create inside jokes and let people in on them.
We plant seeds and let the water run
on a little too long so we can put our feet
in the mud and chase each other
through the yard making rainbows
with the garden hose.

In this family it's ok to be overwhelmed,
angry, and sad. It's ok to need space,
and to watch the same TV show ten times
because it feels safe. We have built our family
on unconventional models of freedom
and safety, letting our love of each other,
not of the rules, be our guide.

Motherhood

Today I will watch you hold the violin
bow so delicately, and every harsh word
I've said will become the shrill
sound of learning
how to place the hair between the
bridge and the fingerboard.

Your face becomes the muscle
memory I will tap out on the
tablecloth when everything else
is forgotten.

Triangle Dreams

Drink deeply of the warm, bitter Heqet and let
the pharaohs enter your bloodstream with their big triangle
dreams and all their feline familiars. Slide downwards

through the false door, past the mummified kings and into
darkened caverns, spelunking to the underworld,
away from the sun's brutal landscape. Soft and wet,

green and fertile, soil and ash. Sanctuary, sanctum.
Sleek muscles move under soft fur. Glowing eyes and
predatory instincts, licking our claws clean of blood

and ruin, we are growing new souls out of the piles
of fur in the corner. We are creating a golem
of fingernails and the hair that gets caught in the Roomba.

In the shadows gather the parts of myself that I
no longer need. The piece who appeases her mother,
who seeks her approval, begs for her attention.

The piece who crumbles into statuesque disrepair
at the casual abandonments of her father,
the relief of his death, the grief of relief.

Will they pick up our discarded pieces and put
them in a display case with the other strange relics
they aren't sure what to do with? Our lost selves,

on a pedestal next to the giant suits of armor
and the red bisque pots.

The Green Lion

I crave the summer of summer,
the deepest part of heat and life.

I eat the sun, transform into something
green and miraculous,
a slowly unfurling fiddle head,
a strawberry moon

dappled light and a vase full of marigolds,
a wooden window painted in peeling teal

I run until I become a ghost of lace
and filtered sunlight,
a subtle dust of ecstasy.

Leave me here in the
height of summer,
leave me here
with my pockets full
and my grief undone.

Dream Language

I've swallowed the sun
and it burns like a broken heart
in the late desert snake heat.

I don't know why I'm
always being tasked
with impossible things,

like carrying an entire
universe in my chest,

but they call me a shapeshifter,
and I become the panther

and then the bear, the dragonfly,
the slick frog, and the sunset fox.

I'm not sure if it's all metaphor
or truth beyond the
confines of a narrative mind,

but I awake more empowered
and less confused, alive to something
that never stays the same,

asks nothing
and everything of me.

Shapeshifter

Stop trying so hard,
release control,
your palms are filled with emptiness,
yet everything good has a season.

Let everything that has died
become the compost for your next love.
Spread ashes around the rose bushes.

Plant something new.
Sit quietly on the front porch
and survey the growing things.
Don't rush the harvest.
Don't ignore the splendor.

Who was I?

Alive and wolven,
I was a small creature howling,
making her way through
the din of the city streets,
dangerous and in danger,
fanged, but also hunted.

I was ten different kinds of survival.

I was be the good daughter survival
and be the quiet kid survival
I was be appreciative survival
and take care of myself survival
I was don't tell the whole truth survival
and create a back up plan survival
I was make another plan for the back-up plan
and hang a rope out the window survival
create a family of my friends survival
and be the smartest, prettiest, funniest, most laid-back survival.

Who was I before the mechanisms?
I'm just beginning to see.
I'm just remembering my fangs.

For a minute there, I lost myself

If anyone needs me
I'll be reverting to my
14-year-old self with
41-year-old wisdom.

Making giant wall collages
and listening to Radiohead,
cutting up old t-shirts
and putting them back
together with safety pins.

Questioning everything
I've been taught.

Finding new friends,
owning my weird,
wearing giant moon earrings,
and dreaming of taking
psychedelics on a perfect
summer evening.

Going to see bands no one
has ever heard of, showing
up for my friends' art shows
and poetry readings,
clapping a little too loudly.

Endlessly browsing
Barnes & Noble for my
newest identity,

shopping in the cheap make-up
aisle for the
exact shade of lipstick
to sell the world
on my adulthood.

A flood of doors

We are so small compared to the sky and so
large compared to our memories.
I can never remember the exact shape of your
mouth, but I touch it with my fingertips
each night.

Some day, I will be nothing but these notebooks,
these strange metaphors, this broken wand.

I write about the moment I
break open, and in doing so,
I forget how to maintain the opening,
become a flood of doors.

Don't ask me to become the Moon

She is gigantic with the light of
someone else and cold to the touch,
and even though she is enough
(she is always enough),

I would rather be a mound of warm
dirt teeming with life, writhing with
the rise and fall of decay and rebirth.

I spent too long as something that shined,
and now I just want to be something
that lives forever, in pieces,
in conversation with the trees.

What do I do?

I read when I can
I make lunch for my son
I put my feet in the earth
I pick up leaves
and trace fingers down the veins.

I notice subtle changes in the air
I smile at the moon
I remember to breathe, to pay attention
I carve out time for my friends
I listen, I listen, I listen.

I allow connections to form in my mind,
I honor them, I believe in them
I remember to breathe
I remember to smile.

I take a drive
look at your face, read your expressions,
ask gentle questions
I listen for truth
I make art of lies.

I take momentary
emotions and carve
a river through the middle of them,
make of them two mountains facing each other
as the orange sun sets over the pink stones.

I harbor memory.

I press my cheek to
the chest of the world, run my fingers
down the spine, and pray
we will hear where it hurts.

A nameless thing

I am trying to find you/me/
the thing that can only exist
between us
give it a name
a shape perhaps.

It fits inside my palm
like your cheek.
It fits inside your chest
like a breath
and I am always trying

to find a way to hold it
closer. I am always trying
to remember
what it's called.

Identities

I'm an artist first,

gulping down beauty
until it won't fit inside my form

until it's overflowing onto
the shag carpeting

everything damp with silver
everyone's mouths hanging open,

agape.

Simple Things

I wrap myself in simple things:
in daily walks and easy conversations,
in loose clothes and sunlight,
in mindless TV and social media.

I wrap myself in ritual
to keep the world at bay,
measure out the sugar, the sweet cream, the tea,
the specific kind of heat that brings
my heart to a boil.

I wrap myself in moonlight and evening shade.
I tend to those around me,
try on new little things,
but one at a time
one at a time.

41

I am 41 and scared,
not of being bad or losing it all,
not of drinking again or messing up,

but of this beautiful life we've made
and how it could put me to sleep again,

lull me into oblivion where the years pass like dreams,
and one day soon I know it'll all be behind me.

And perhaps thais is how joy feels,
like a quickening.

And so I pause and breathe into the fear
and the beautiful realization
that it doesn't get much better than this.

Finally

I clean my office and buy some house plants.
I almost believe I'll keep them alive.
I'm learning to name my needs
before I wear them between my teeth, growling.

I'm no longer of afraid of saying no
or losing people who can't honor my limits.

My heart is a jaguar who knows where to go,
and I have finally begun to listen to her first.

Rabbits in the fog

A doe nuzzles me as I stand in a vast meadow,
purple with dawn and fog.
Everything is soft and misty and quiet,
a blanket of calm.

I look out and see colonies of rabbits
all facing me, dotting the field
to the horizon, where I can just make out
a black panther through the mist.

"What does it mean?" I ask the deer
"We're all here with you, it's just a moment
of fog," she replies.

Fog's Message

There is no perfect path to follow
only beautiful, unfolding options.

Do some work to understand
your ambitions and get clarity
on your dreams.

What if you're not dreaming big enough?
Allow yourself to desire,
long for new things.

Stop hiding behind façades
and shine your essence into the world.

The pleasure of attention

I look down at my own hands
extending from within a navy blue robe,
typing gently on black keys
as the cat beside me tries to
burrow her head under my right arm.

My fingers toggle between document
and model, the words emerging slowly,
my mind searching for a metaphor
like a child trying to find his
missing shoe.

Full of the pink promise
of distraction, my phone buzzes
in my lap. Inside it are unanswered texts
and social media notifications,
the sweet lure of mindless videos,
and post-work conversations;
a world inside a world.

I resist the urge to open it
and turn instead to the soft
static of my mind, the subtle pain
in my neck, the warmth of
the cat and the steady hum of her purrs.

The ticking of the ceiling fan
is a rhythmic background for
the distant cackle of my son's laughter,
a domestic song I so easily
could have missed.

Making friends as an adult

I'm no wiser, but I'm older
and with that comes a certain
kind of certainty:
    that love is perennial,
    that rest will eventually add up to enough,
    that kindness is never wasted,
    and being weird is just about
the best and most courageous way
to make friends for life.

There are two kinds of mornings:

The kind where I can't wait to taste the coffee,
put my feet in the soil, kiss my partner, hug my child,
put pen to paper, listen to the doves having their early
conversations in the treetops.

And the kind where my heart feels like lead and everything hurts.
When I can't shake the anxiety dreams
and everyone feels loud and impossible.

The mornings when everyone seems to be doing yard-work
and the world is heavy with grief I can feel in my hips.

And today has been both, the heavy and the light,
the impossibly beautiful and the impossibly sad.

As I get older, the space between grief and joy has disappeared
and everything has become a new and complex flavor,
a bittersweet masterpiece of love and loss,
of longing and profound gratitude.

Saturday

The sound of my son
rises up from the living room
and my neurotic cat cries
outside my closed office door.

The world is requesting my presence
with a Saturday kind of slow,
and for now, my breath is as steady
as the slowly drifting clouds.

What do you believe in?

I believe in mornings,
in the soft way the sun breaks
like a yolk over the horizon,
the momentary stillness,
the ease of movement,
the sharp smell of dawn.

I believe in the familiarity
two souls can feel in an instant,
the way some people just look like home,
their bone structure the exact shape
of the moon the night you were born.

I believe in a kind of energy that never dies,
that lives on and on,
first in oxygen, then in pine needles,
the mycelium breathing information to the roots.
The eldest child passing down secrets to the youngest.

I believe in patterns, in divine timing,
and trusting your body.
I believe in quitting things
you no longer want to do
and lovingly letting go of relationships
that don't honor your wholeness.

I believe in change, in flow,
in water and air and fire and earth.
I believe in the alchemy of friendship
and the austerity of the time when the pen
becomes your only lifeline.

I believe in a beauty that rises in the darkness,
not as a light,
but as a deeper kind of black.

Rain

The ground is slick with beauty,
my jaw is sore with worry,
and all of the good words have been said.
I sigh and drink my tea.
I stretch and listen to the rain.
I try not to hope too much for things.
I try not to despair.

War

War has begun
and it feels familiar
in my cells
like this dread is a deep
and wretched
part of being human.
I am a mother
desperate to hold my child.
I am a soldier moving
toward the rising smoke.
I am the land
prepared for devastation,
ready to hold the blood
memories for decades,
the sunflowers
the soil
the hope that
one day soon
it won't come to this.

Prayer

If only we could just make
the smallest dent in
all this cruelty
without becoming cruel
ourselves in the process.

Resolutions

Resolve only to
breathe more freely
more deeply
more soundly
into your own
sweet aliveness

What I don't show on social media

My uneven red winter skin
My son running around in his underwear
The dedication, persistence, and patience of my husband.
The unraked leaves, the unmown grass,
the intense glares from the neighbors.
I don't show you how much energy it takes for me to get dressed
or smile or follow through on plans.

I don't show anyone in the multitude of cancellations
or how my body refuses to do even one more little thing.
The piles of La Croix cans, my replacements for alcohol,
the way I have to remind myself to unclench my jaw
and breathe more deeply every few minutes.

I don't show you my expired car registration
or the 6,000 miles overdue it is to be serviced.
I don't show you the stack of unpaid tolls, the water bills.
The bank fees I could avoid if I simply made the phone call
I've been saying I would for four years.

I don't show you the closet full of clothes
that don't quite fit anymore because I'm going to start working out
and eating less macaroni and cheese. Any minute now.
I don't show you the brief conversations I have with myself
in the mirror, naked, and alone, when I remind myself, how loved I am,
how enough and not too much at once.

When I smile like a mother would at her child
and say, "Don't worry, love, one day it'll all come easier to you.
I love you just as you are,"
before I sink into the second bath of the day
with a quiet, childlike sigh.

Women's Work

He is crying, head in hands,
and I am watching him from
the arm of the couch,
a little out of body.

I am angry and scared of losing him,
but probably, if I'm more honest, more
scared of losing myself in my attempt to stay.

We are in the middle of a conversation
we've had four times recently.
I ask for more attention,
and he apologizes for not doing anything right.

We both feel unheard.

I am up here, watching him cry
and wondering how to get my needs met
while also meeting his for the 9 billionth time.

Being a woman is so damned unfair sometimes,
the way we're conditioned to think of ourselves
in relation to the well-being of others.

How even my sadness,
my grief,
my anger,
my loneliness,
becomes a problem I'm solving for him.

Hornet's Message

My anger is a kind of insect,
emerging as a swarm of hornets,
flying unannounced
from the deepest parts of my gullet.

I could warn you there will be months when smiling
is as hard as lifting an entire rack of free weights,
when I think I'm smiling but really it's the face
of a spring-up clown: Unwanted. Terrifying.

I could warn you that the way I love is
just as frightening as the anger and depression.
It will cling to your arm and wail, trying
to hold on to the moment, to make it cinematic,
to hold it still.

I could warn you that I'm never just one thing,
but you wouldn't believe me.
That's the way it works.
You see, in a singular dimension,
everything looks coherent.

But tilt me sideways, love,
squint your eyes and look for the hidden secret;
it'll say, *I warned you.*
But like everyone else,

you couldn't hear me over all these bees,
over all these oceans of selves,
humming, changing, and disappearing,
like smoke.
an unholdable magic. a ghost.

Invent something new

A machine that will
record your dream poems,
the ones that evaporate
with the morning dew.

Invent a way to eat well
without having to cook
or order in food.

A way to go hiking
 and also sit on the couch,
 eating popcorn and playing Zelda.

Invent a way to ask for help
that doesn't involve
the possibility of more loss
or more pain.

The January of never-ending grays

And the sky was gunmetal gray
in the January of never-ending grays.
I sat hypnotized, mesmerized by the gathering snow,
fatigued and uninspired,
all coffee-brained and sleep deprived—
all this privilege does nothing to help me rest.

How many winters have I disappeared
into the bare bones of myself?

Barely able to move this body through space,
barely able to form intelligible sentences?

And what does it mean to be completely undone every year?
The snowstorm mutes the pain: A righteous, quieting numb.

See, the paper takes the ink. My hand
holds the pen, my arm holds the hand, and even now,
I am a woman. And I am not.

Forgiveness

The light bouncing off the half-frozen lake
reminds me to be gentler with myself

to let the soft rays of the sun
become my salvation

to weaken the parts that have become hard
with grief and exhaustion.

Slowly relax my cells until they bend again
into water

until I forgive myself
for having been so cold.

Normal is overrated

I have never felt this close to belonging,
never before really found my people,
though everyone knows I've searched.

I looked in churches and dance clubs,
in Dungeons & Dragons games,
and dark Chicago bars.

I looked on OkCupid and found
more loneliness, swiping into
boring conversations.

What do normal people even talk about?

I want to know if you think time is real,
if you've lived a thousand lives
or are currently living infinite ones simultaneously.
I want to know if you loved your father,
and how did it feel to have him love you back?

Can you describe how your distaste
for your neighbors rises in your throat
like indigestion and how you spend some nights
fantasizing about your best friend's brother?

I've always wanted to know the underneath things,
how people talk to themselves in the car
on the way home from a party.
What does your inner monologue
sound like? And does she know
how magical you are?

Do you know how magical you are?

When the Sun sets at 4pm

Time moves faster
than my soul
in winter.

I barely wake
and it is night
again.

Projects fall behind
and I sit with my
fresh brew

and ponder just
how gray the sky
can be.

Sunday

What I want is to wake
to the sound of the mourning dove cooing,
the smell of freshly cut lawn and pancakes
frying on the griddle.

I want to pour the syrup thick
without once thinking about the size
of my body

only the sweetness
of Sunday.

Bohème

(after Mathias Svalina)

Take the words and fold them
into a paper accordion.

Take a knife and stab through the middle
until the poem is just the hearts of paper dolls.

Unfold your hearts and spread them on the table.
Wipe the blood off on a napkin
and remember the opera where Mimi dies of consumption,

but she sings,
she sings with blood in her throat,
she sings as they freeze in an apartment in Paris.

Burn the chairs, burn the manuscript.
The ashes are the poem.

Read the poem to the empty bed.
Scatter the ashes under her favorite tree,
eat the fruit it bears,
red juice dripping down your chin.

Begin again,
this time as the sun,
this time as the sun.

Hermit Season

I'm learning how to trust the season,
myself, the achy, awful slowness
that eventually turns to some kind of
peaceful acceptance.

My body becomes an open door
with darkness on the other side.
I move slowly and with no guidance,
disoriented,

hand on the wall of change.
I will emerge and so will you,
and not the same as before.

Winter's Message

This winter is teaching me what enough is,
how it feels to allow a sense of worthiness to exist
even when productivity is not on the menu.
I'm learning when and how to force myself
out of the house for my own mental health and
when playing an hour of video games before
my son comes home is the right call.

I'm learning I can show up for myself,
I can hold my sad heart, deep in my chest,
and let her be heavy and sore.
I can survive my own grief.

When all is cold

Turn toward the things that warm you:
The sun, a cup of Lady Gray,
the dog with his small dog sighs,
the cat who settles in just as you need more coffee.
Memories, cookies, soup,
the future in which we live more collectively.
Root vegetables,
tiny bookstores with a bell at the entrance.
Large coffee shops with couches and table lamps,
conversations about people you love,
the soft pants, the made bed,
the train ticket to Montreal.
The road trip, the old atlas
with every place you've been marked in red.

To be missed

I needed a place to hold me.
I needed somewhere big enough
for all four limbs, all five hearts,
all the multitudes of antlers and branches.

I needed you to see me,
but I was standing on the dark side
of the street lamp,
I was calling out from under the train,
I was whistling while the tea kettle sang,

and every part of me was drowned out
by the noise of the world.

I took myself down to the river
and lay prone in the water and waited,
waited for you to miss me.
And not because I was going
to do something for you.

Not because I didn't make dinner
or didn't read you a book
But because you missed the way
I break things down
into multiple-part stories,
beginning with who was there
and where we were.

Because I cry when anything
gets at a truth too hard to name
with normal language.
Because I am a woman
who waited in the water,
with the stars and the silence
to be remembered.

Wind's Message

Move toward big feelings
Open doors
Magic.

A list of things to remember

Most of the time you can meet your own needs.
Walking in the woods solves more problems than you'd think.
Our hearts synchronize when we sing.
Your inner voice is not cruel, cruelty's voice is always someone else.
Animals know things.
We are animals.
We can sense the rain, a storm, the change of seasons.
We have a symbiotic relationship with plants - we need each other to survive.
Rest and time fix many, many things.
It is not too late for you to love your life.

A list of other important things (in no particular order)

Gravity: the way the Earth holds us all close,
the simple magnetic pull toward warmth and safety.

Reflection: the ability to hold a contradiction,
a paradox, to be both separate from one another and as one.
To love by letting everyone be exactly as they are.

Travel: the pilgrimage, the going away and coming back,
the hardship, the desert vision,
the long, slow, road back to yourself.

Forgiveness: of the self primarily, of disconnection and selfishness,
of overextension and restlessness.
Of your mother, your father, your gods, and your children.

Transformation: a dying to old ways,
a reclaiming of that which returns again and again,
resurrection, redemption, reconciliation, rebirth.
Vitality and youth, the wisdom of tender things.

Transformation

They say it's like a moth cocooned,
but it's more like a TV being turned off
six hours after everyone else
went to bed.

More like walking onto a set
in the middle of the night
and losing all sense of day and time,
your life suddenly scripted
by an LA director who brunches
at a place with $32 French toast.

It's more like a diner in Neodesha, Kansas,
where anyone might be a second cousin,
where half the graves at the cemetery
carry your last name,
where everyone looks vaguely familiar
but no one knows your name.

It's a lot more like flying the red-eye back
from Amsterdam and knowing
you have to end your college relationship because
who you were feels like a far-off school bell,

a class dismissed for the summer,
petals falling suddenly
and completely from the cherry tree.

Spring's Message

I can feel my energy stirring,
twitching, turning,
little tendrils of aliveness
waking in the dark.

A slow, sly smile
rising from the depths -
I am here.

Sagittarius Rising

I've spent so many days in my own company
I keep forgetting I can just drive downtown and
see something new.

I live for brightly painted canvases and eclectic little thrift stores.
I can buy myself mint chip ice cream and watch
the pigeons watching me for waffle cone crumbs.

I can call a friend or walk the dog or open a new document.
I can change genres; I can change my name,
move to Scotland and work in a tavern, wake every morning
to sheep and clover fields, take notes on the townspeople,
make my way toward Asia on the train.

I've locked myself in a pattern that felt like safety
and boredom, kept the water hot for tea, the
house clean for company. But the Sagittarius in me
is screaming for a new set of rules, a new playlist
full of songs I love, and an adventure pouring
out in front of me.

The Archer's Message

We need to spend less time in front of screens
and more time in front of fires,
wandering the pine-lined paths,
in downtown coffee shops, and small town bookstores.

Hug your friends and sing in harmony,
go to music shows and speak at open mics.
Travel by train and remind yourself
that the world is meant to be moved through.

Ancestral Lands

There are horses
there are drums
there is singing and laughter
I can see for miles
ocean, meadow, moors
I am safe.

Cicada Years

All this to say, I'm coming out of my shell,
and all the other clichés about things that
shed their skin because they've outgrown
themselves. Perhaps I *should* sit screaming
on a branch for a season or two. Become
the train whistle, the warning bell, the
loudest kind of shrieking. When we are in
danger, shouldn't we say so? Why are we all
so quiet? All this to say, I've been waiting
for this reckoning.

Pine Tree's Message

I wandered off,
finally setting down my phone,
and turning to the inward parts
of myself for a long and winding chat.
To ask how I'm handling things,
to see if there might be some needs
I haven't noticed.

I walked past my favorite pine
with her red bark rising
up into a halo of greens,
and stood beneath the
cathedral of branches to listen
for an answer.

"Take your time with this," she answered.
"Don't try to drink all the water at once.
Take breaks and lay, uneventfully
in the sun. Let your heart rate slow
and the evening come,
and don't fill every day with purpose.

Trust your guts; they twist
and turn when you've crossed
a line, but also trust the warm
rush of joy.

Trust the energy that has felt
so elusive; it is real.
It is yours.
It is safe to play with,
to occupy,
to use as wings."

Sparrow's Message

The thing is, to change your life
requires no giant shift,
though giant shifts are welcome.
Each day becomes a window
slightly more open to possibility.
Each time you say yes to your values,
you hear the birdsong of a better kind of world
more clearly.

When the light comes back on

My god, I forgot
how good it feels
to want something,

to be awakened
in the most
inside places,

a tiny doorway
is shining light
down a hallway,

somewhere so deep
within me,
I didn't know
it existed.

The Overture

A startling opening,
a symphony of color and lust
for sunlight.

This spring is a melody
I've been writing in my head
for years. Playing over
and over until I forget
I made it up myself.

I try to figure out where I've heard it before,
somewhere long ago;
down the hallway of my first
church or around the fire at camp.

Somewhere green and easy,
and full of song.

Sunlight's Message

Move toward fresh fruit
Bare feet
Laughter.

Lakeside

We walk to the lake
and read Walt Whitman
aloud in silly voices, our own
absurdity making us giggle
with delight.

The ducks take notice
of our glee and swim
our way in hopes of a handout.
But all we have to offer
is Mary Oliver and our knees
gently touching each other
as we sit on the stairs.

I look at your profile,
highlighted by the setting sun,
and I smile a smile
I haven't felt since I was 12,
a kind of joy that only exists
before anyone has ever
broken your heart.

What has been eclipsed is shifting at last

The earth sings a song of blossoms
and generosity, and I reach
for one more handful
of bread, one more ripe
orange, one more kiss.

My hand on your chest,
pulling you closer
than the full moon
standing watch
outside our window.

I become the insatiable
birdsong, the outrageous
white blossoms against
that blue sky. I open
again, and the world rushes
in like seawater through
the open lock.

Crush

It's indie music and light rain,
it's the song you fell in love with
at 16, played over and over again
the summer you learned how to drive.
It's the smell of tobacco and pine needles,
the feeling of turning off the fluorescent light
the quiet of the body after a long walk in the woods.
It's the exhale of pleasure when your crush
finally touches the inside of your palm,
the sigh of pure joy after peels of laughter.

"You feel so good," I say over and over.
You feel so good.

Marking Time

Tell me about May,
the pink buds and the wet grass,

the colors so bright it's hard to remember
the gray of February.

Time passes differently at 40,
I can taste every hour like honey
not quite dissolved in hot water,

but the months go by as airports do,
unnoticed and liminal.

Soon I will be 41, and then 47 and 52,
The years gathering speed as a wagon does
on the long slope home.

And I mark time in the month of May.

What a gorgeous time to be alive
and slowly dying.

A month when even mortality
smells of pink blossoms.

Crow's Message

Do not be afraid; you couldn't be less alone.
You are everything -
every white-bellied squirrel leaping
every drum beat
every hoof fall
every water droplet
every leaf quivering
You are a map seen from space

Just write it down and speak it aloud.
Don't censor yourself,
don't judge yourself by human standards;
you are not human, you are tree-being,
mud-woman, sky-woman,
poet. Earth-speaker, mountain.
Echo of god.

An Invocation

I call in the power of creativity, reassurance,
the knowledge that everything has a season of dormancy,
and I am lucky to be able to anticipate mine.

I call in friends with oodles of patience, compatriots,
co-conspirators, joy-makers, noise-makers, change-agents,
freedom-fighters, nature-lovers, cozy tea-sippers, and
layabouts.

I embody the spirit of domesticity,
of poetic noncompliance.
I call in restful rebellion and slow,
anti-capitalist beauty -

the kind of beauty you *want* to work for.

Emerging from the cave

Something new is coming
a spark has lit itself
in the deepest parts of your soul
a rumbling has begun
the cracking open is here.

You have strength, stability, enthusiasm, love
you are supported from all sides
everything starts fresh from here
the time to create a new reality
is now.

I am here to try again

to be a person,
to find the person parts
I've left along the way.

Robin's Message

Become the milky doorway,
the red-breasted creature
of the in-between,
the goddess liminal.
Let secrets form the calcium
of your newly formed skeleton;

trust what stays in the bones.

Fat with Joy

I want to come home
and really be there -
a whole me,
resplendent and healthy
and wise with joy.

Fat with joy.
Overflowing with life
and lust
and rebellion.

I want to change the world,
and I want to look back and say,
then.
That was the day,
the week,
the place,
the moment I found out who I could be
and became her.

Multiple Lives

You don't know this, but I've been thinking about running away, cloning myself into three, and creating another set of lives.

The first would stay with you and raise our son. She might even learn how to meal plan and start going to the grocery store again instead of ordering our food from Amazon. She is going to join the Y and lift weights to become strong enough to hike with you forever. She is going to give you evening back rubs and stand outside with you, marveling at the brightness of Venus, and how long the grass is getting.

The second will take her leave and start an art gallery in San Diego. She will buy a small oceanfront bungalow and wake at dawn to put her feet in the Pacific. She will have a nightly Corona with lime and lead drum circles at the tarot shop. She is a teacher and a healer; she wears long skirts and loves to sing. She is free and open and lets stray cats and teenagers live at her house as long as they need to. She has learned to paint and all she paints are the glimpses of your face that come to her unbidden in her dreams.

The third clone is a poetry professor in Paris. She has a small apartment with a balcony and a gorgeous girlfriend who bakes croissants and pan au chocolate at the bakery down the street. She throws small dinner parties and hosts intellectual salons; she is changing the world. She and her lover take the train to Berlin on the weekend and touch each other's lips as the sun sets over the Spree. She has forgotten your name, but sometimes she catches your scent as she passes a grove of oranges, and she is pulled through a portal of remembering.

The end of hibernation

The seasons have their way with you,
and it's summer once again.
You have woken from an accidental
hibernation, starving and achy.

You take your mama bear body to the lake
and drink cold water until you can swallow
freely again, stuff your face with wild salmon
and strawberries, begin the long walk to
rediscover yourself.

Somehow you know it will be winter again
before the cobwebs clear, and you can
already see the calendar pages turning.

This year you are reorienting, building a new
compass from sand and memories.

Next year you will begin again as something new,
something stronger and wiser, something
freer and fiercer, leaner and kinder.

Next year you will find your footing and the visions
will come in crisper, but for now you will allow this
slow stumble to the edges of the known world.

Understand that this is the season you are in,
and every season prepares us for the next.

Thorns

Every time I find myself on the mat,
beating myself senseless with
my own judgment,
I take my body to the woods.

I walk among the gnats and mosquitoes;
I bask in the dark green sunlight
and walk until the voices become
my footsteps,

quiet and rhythmic.

I walk until I love myself again,
until the earth reminds me that
every living thing has a stinger
or a barb,

that survival isn't always sweet
and self-protection is an
inevitable consequence of
sharing breath with a sometimes
hostile world.

I walk until I become the rose or
the milk thistle,
thorny yet beautiful,
allowed to hurt sometimes.
Allowed to demand more space to grow.

My body knows what heals it

A dark room and cool rain tapping on the roof,
an uninterrupted view to the horizon.
being fully heard.
curiosity,
love,
the simple act of creation,
be it drawing, photography, poetry,
or life.

My body knows what heals it,
and mostly it's the simplest of things:
the sun,
my own sweet, unconditional love,
and time
to make something beautiful and true.

Initiate yourself into the world of magical things   4
Poet Seer   5
House Cat Days   6
Jaguar Nights   7
What is magic?   8
Taurus Sun   9
I Tried   10
What do you want?   11
Cave of Arrows   12
I take selfies when I'm depressed   13
The Midsummer Fairy   14
Litha   15
Dream Lemons   16
Cowboys   17
My Roman Empire   18
A New Archetype   19
Why Poetry?   20
A song plays unexpectedly on Spotify   21
Buck Moon   22
That kind of summer   23
Brooding   24
Fallow   25
Be here now   26
The planets are scrambling my mind   27
Close   28
The Seeker   29
Snow White   30
12 Dancing Princesses   31
Artifacts   32
Wiser   33
Matriarch   34
The Other World   35
River Song   36
Everything Good   37
Embodiment has its perks   38
The Hum   39
Chosen Family   40
Motherhood   41
Triangle Dreams   42
The Green Lion   43
Dream Language   44
Shapeshifter   45

Who was I?   46
For a minute there, I lost myself   47
A flood of doors   48
Don't ask me to become the Moon   49
What do I do?   50
A nameless thing   51
Identities   52
Simple Things   53
41   54
Finally   55
Rabbits in the fog   56
Fog's Message   57
The pleasure of attention   58
Making friends as an adult   59
There are two kinds of mornings: 60
Saturday   61
What do you believe in?   62
Rain   63
War   64
Prayer   65
Resolutions   66
What I don't show on social media   67
Women's Work   68
Hornet's Message   69
Invent something new   70
The January of never-ending grays   71
Forgiveness   72
Normal is overrated   73
When the Sun sets at 4pm   74
Sunday   75
Bohème   76
Hermit Season   77
Winter's Message   78
When all is cold   79
To be missed   80
Wind's Message   81
A list of things to remember   82
A list of other important things (in no particular order)   83
Transformation   84
Spring's Message   85
Sagittarius Rising   86
The Archer's Message   87

Ancestral Lands   88
Cicada Years   89
Pine Tree's Message   90
Sparrow's Message   91
When the light comes back on   92
The Overture   93
Sunlight's Message   94
Lakeside   95
What has been eclipsed is shifting at last   96
Crush   97
Marking Time   98
Crow's Message   99
An Invocation   100
Emerging from the cave   101
I am here to try again   102
Robin's Message   103
Fat with Joy   104
Multiple Lives   105
The end of hibernation   106
Thorns   107
My body knows what heals it   108

Made in United States
Troutdale, OR
07/11/2024

21160770R00072